21 Days of 2021

Melissa Li

BookLeaf
Publishing

India | USA | UK

Presentation by *BookLeaf Publishing*

Web: www.bookleafpub.com

E-mail: info@bookleafpub.com

ISBN:

First edition 2022

Preface

These poems are a challenge for myself, a push to step out of my comfort zone. I sincerely hope those who read this can add their own additions and changes on the pages. Thank you.

Acknowledgement

Thank you to everyone who has shown me the joys and wonder of putting my thoughts to paper.

Hellos

Hello to the Sun
Hello to the sky
Hello with a stretch and a great big sigh
Hello to me
and hello to you
Hello and welcome,
what shall we do?

teachers

Mum taught me to care
Dad taught me to laugh

Grandpa taught me patience
Grandma taught me love

My sister taught me to think
My brother taught me to fight

Fight for what you believe in
Fight for what is right

Ms M taught me to read
Ms S taught me to spell

Mr H taught me to keep going until my body
gives out
G. Ravenhall and Madame taught me to have
passion and life

My peers taught me to be humble
My friends taught me to be confident

There's still so much to learn
so who will it be?

Who is my next teacher
I can't wait to see

What if

What if the moon disappeared,
and the stars fell out of the sky.
What if the oceans dried up,
the depths laid bare for our eyes.
What if the winds didn't blow
and the rivers didn't flow.
What if Mount Everest crumbled to the ground
and ice forms instead of melts.
Is the answer to all our problems
if we just stopped asking questions?

Changes

becoming more extroverted
more intuitive and connected
connected with my emotions and feelings and
self
becoming less judgmental
less stressed and scared

changes can be painful and hard to endure
but changes are needed so we can be more

Rainbow ice cream

red yellow orange green and blue
in a bright pink cup with a matching spoon
red yellow orange green and blue
a childhood of simpler things
fairy tales, dolls and play

little bit blue

somedays you just feel a bit blue
you try to smile but just can't shake it off
a good night's sleep and some time for yourself
you'll be okay
somedays you just feel a little bit blue

Courage

C-O-U-R-A-G-E
Courage is different for you and me
For you it's being brave and fighting evil
That is much too scary for cowards like me

C-O-U-R-A-G-E
Courage is different for you and me
For me it's saying, "I'm afraid" with my chin
up and standing tall
That is enough for cowards like me

Fears

Fears are scary and a little bit strange
Vampires, ghosts, zombies galore
Is that a spider in my bathroom?
Nope, no way
See ya I'm out

What next

click click click
another movie or a seven season show
maybe a documentary or a mystery to solve
click click click
what to watch next …

Thank you

Thank you to everyone
Thank you thank you thank you

A little thank you can go a long way
So if you haven't heard it yet today
I just want to say
Thank you for just being you

Hot Chocolate

12

There's the ding of the bell and the coffee I smell
slices of cakes and bread freshly baked
What will it be, a flat white, a mocha, or maybe some tea
cappuccino, frappuccino, latte, hmm I don't know
maybe a long black... yeah, maybe not
Could I get a Hot Chocolate, Extra Hot.

uncertainty

not sure what to write next
not sure what to eat
not sure what to do when there's free time at
my feet
not sure about the present
not sure about what's next
a little bit of uncertainty and …

a little thing called love

Love is warm
Love is kind
Love is heartache
Love is heartbreak
Love is that fuzzy feeling
Love is crying in your pillow because you
care
Love is truly everywhere

Lost or Found

I lost something today
something important, something I need
maybe I left it on my bed, or maybe I left it in
the car
it's not on my desk, it's not on my shelves
it's not in my phone and it's not in my books

Where could it be?
Worry and Fear are staring at me.
They're ready to pounce -- no, NO
give me some time, I'll find it I'm sure

I go to the mirror to take another look
and what do you know
There she is
patiently waiting and looking back at me
"I thought I'd lost you"
"Maybe just for a moment, from some searching
and discoveries"
I chuckle and nod
Looks like we both knew that I'd find her after
all

A letter

Dear

I hope this letter finds you well. I hope your day has been just swell. How are you feeling? Are you okay?

So much has happened in the world and so much has changed. People stayed in their homes for days on end, and the animals took hold of the world outside.

The grey smokey skies cleared into blue and white fluffy clouds dotted the skies. The world around us thrives and we have learnt to cherish the importance of connections.

But the events of 2021 have taken a toll on our bodies and minds. I hope you're okay. I hope you understand. You're not alone. Never. Even when you feel like no one would notice if you were gone. Someone will.

I hope this letter has found you well. I hope
you're feeling just as swell. I look forward
to the tales you'll tell in your letter back.

With all my love

Tears

the sky cries and weeps
the clouds come to join
like cotton wool soaking up the pains of the sky

but after tears come laughter
a rainbow appears
it reminds us that joy comes after the tears

Darn Red Sock

In goes the load ready to wash
Wait a minute, what's that?
Aha! There's my missing red wool sock

Who am I

I am strong
I am brave
I am weak
I am small
I am caring
I am annoying
I am free
I am bound
I can think
I can feel
But sometimes I don't
I make mistakes
I correct them
I hope and I dream
I hate and I love
I am the ocean
I am the sky
I am the trees
I am the earth
I can be whatever I imagine to be

Clouds

aren't they amazing
so many things
dreams and marshmallows
rain and storm
where lightning strikes and thunder roars
yet birds also fly there and soar without a
care
turbulent and calm
white, grey and pink
aren't they amazing
to be so many things

Twenty Questions

What colour is your favourite
What food do you like
What keeps you awake and thinking at night
What would you say to the man on the moon
What would you do if there were no rules
Who would you be in your wildest dreams
Who would you see for even a glance
Who was your first love and are they your
last
Who cheers you up when you're feeling a
tad blue
Who are you in 2021 and who will you be in
2022
Where would you go if you could fly like
the birds
Where do you call home no matter where
you roam
Where is the joy where is the pain
Where are your dreams and are they same
Where are you now in 2021 and where will
you go in 2022
Why do we feel and why do we bleed
Why do we care and why do we speak

Why are we so different yet still all the same
Why so many questions
well... Why not?

And Goodbyes

Goodbye to the Moon
Goodbye to the stars
Goodbye with a yawn, I won't wake until dawn
Goodbye dear friends
but not for long
tomorrow
why don't we have that sing-a-long?

About the Author

Melissa is a lifelong student, with a passion for literature. Putting pen to paper and words on the page, writing is a way for thoughts to come alive.